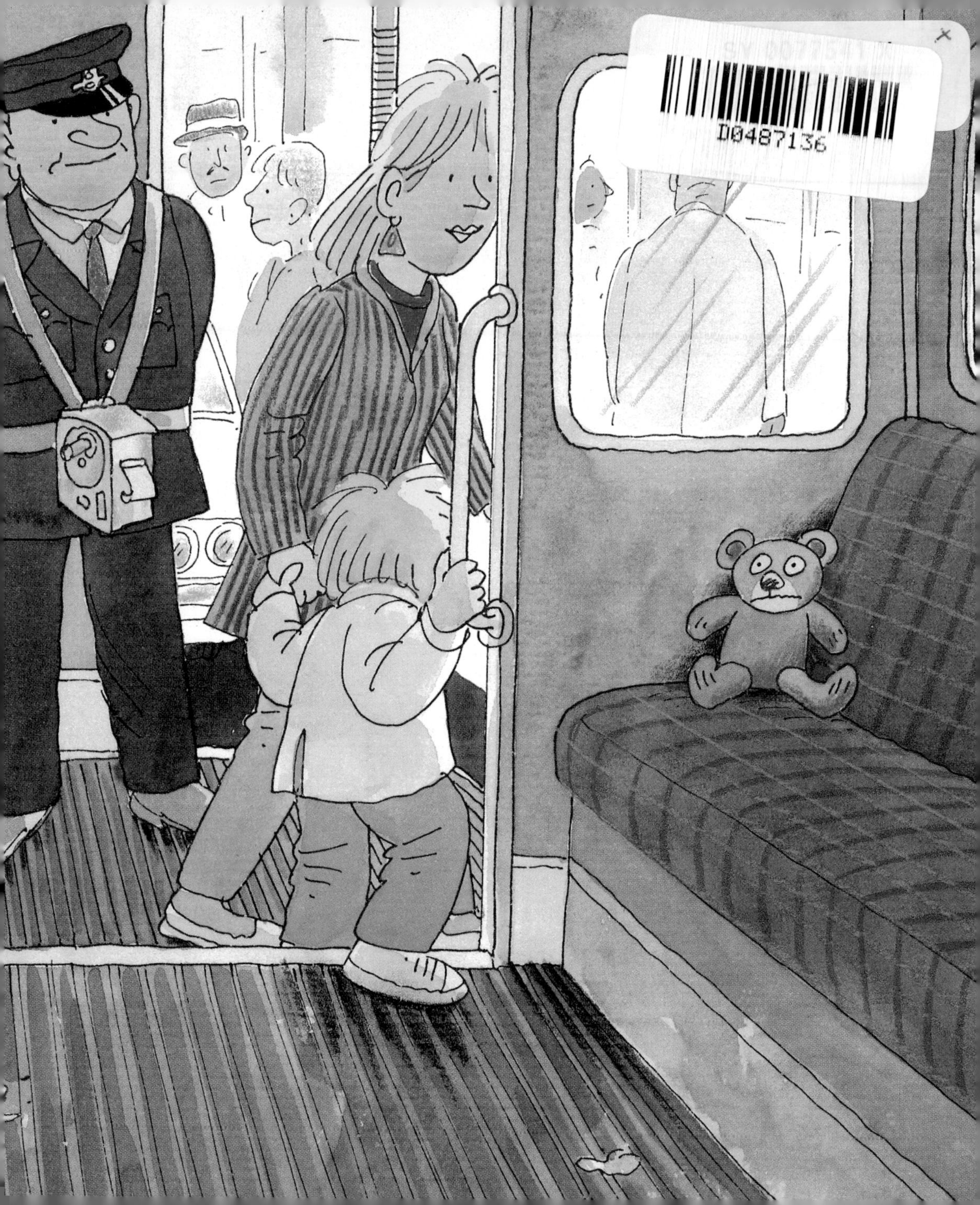

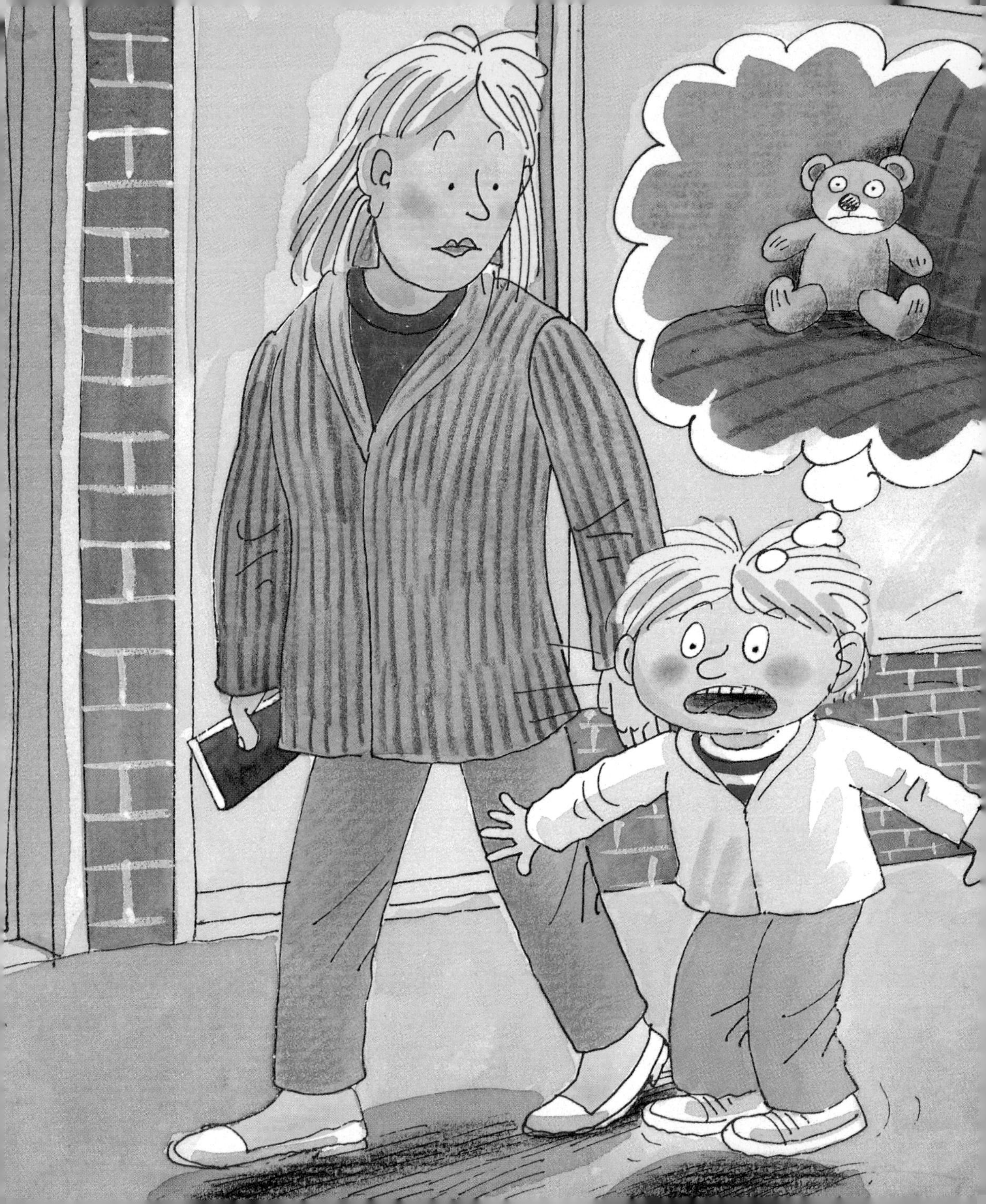

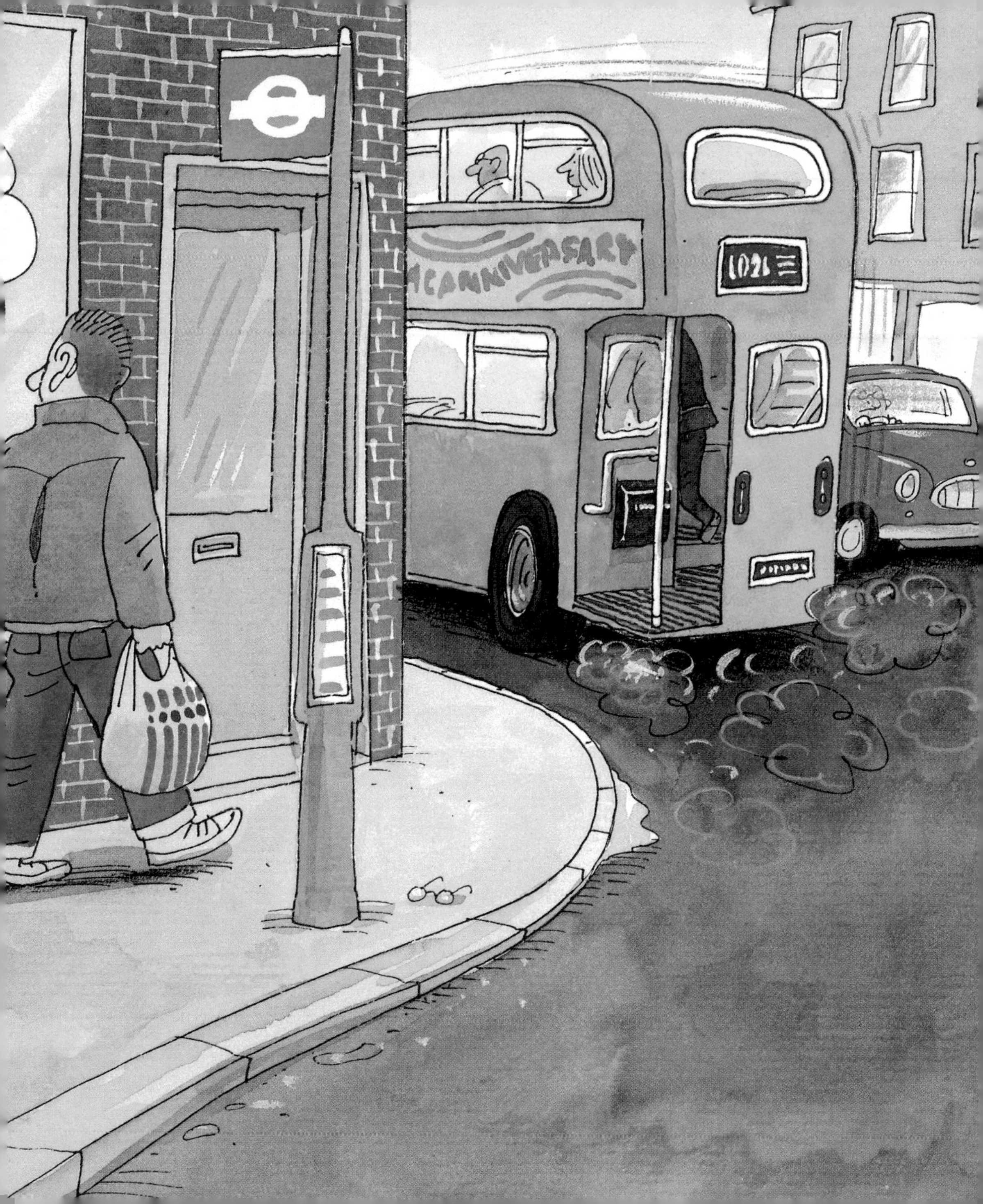
ANNIVERSARY
1026

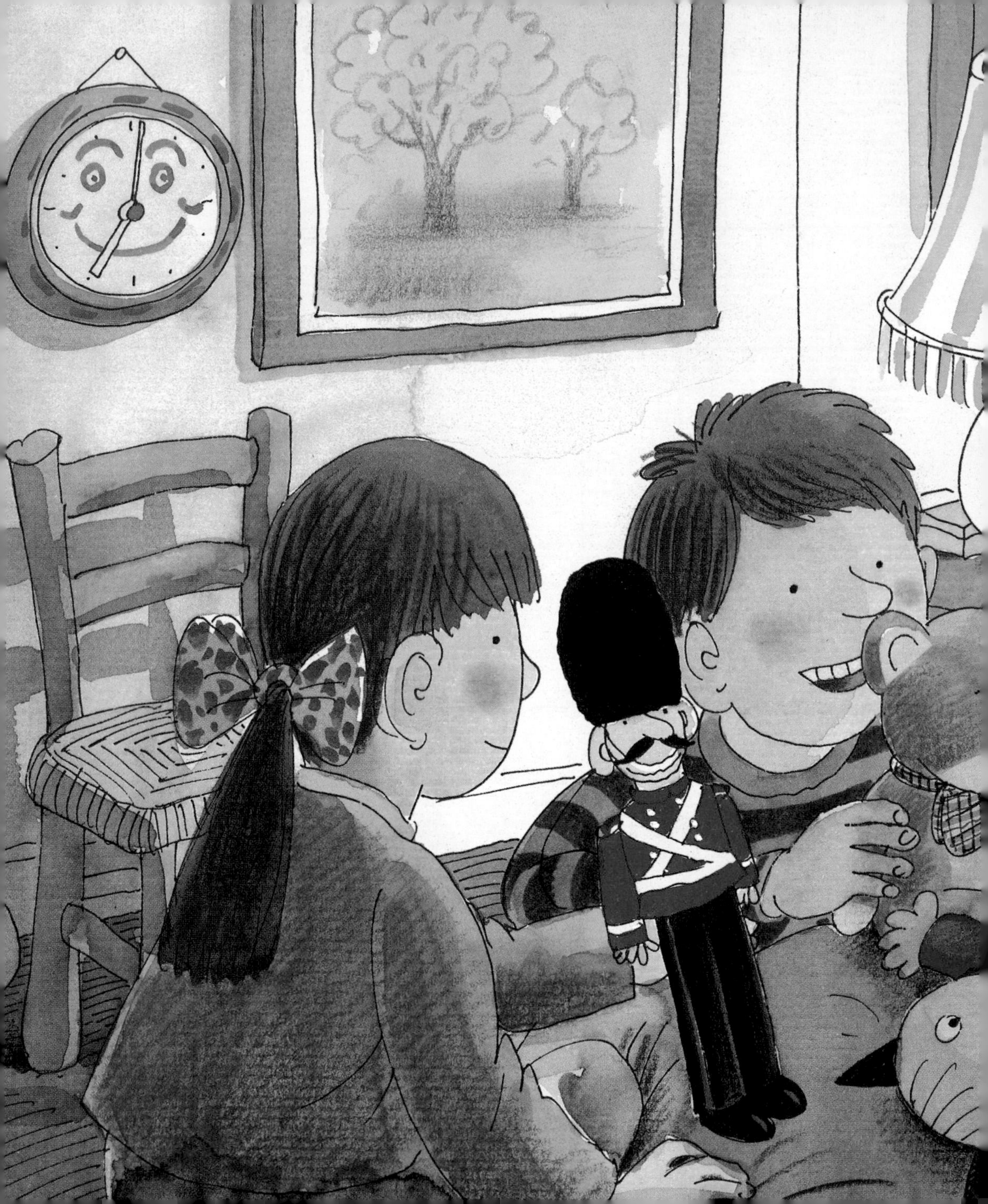

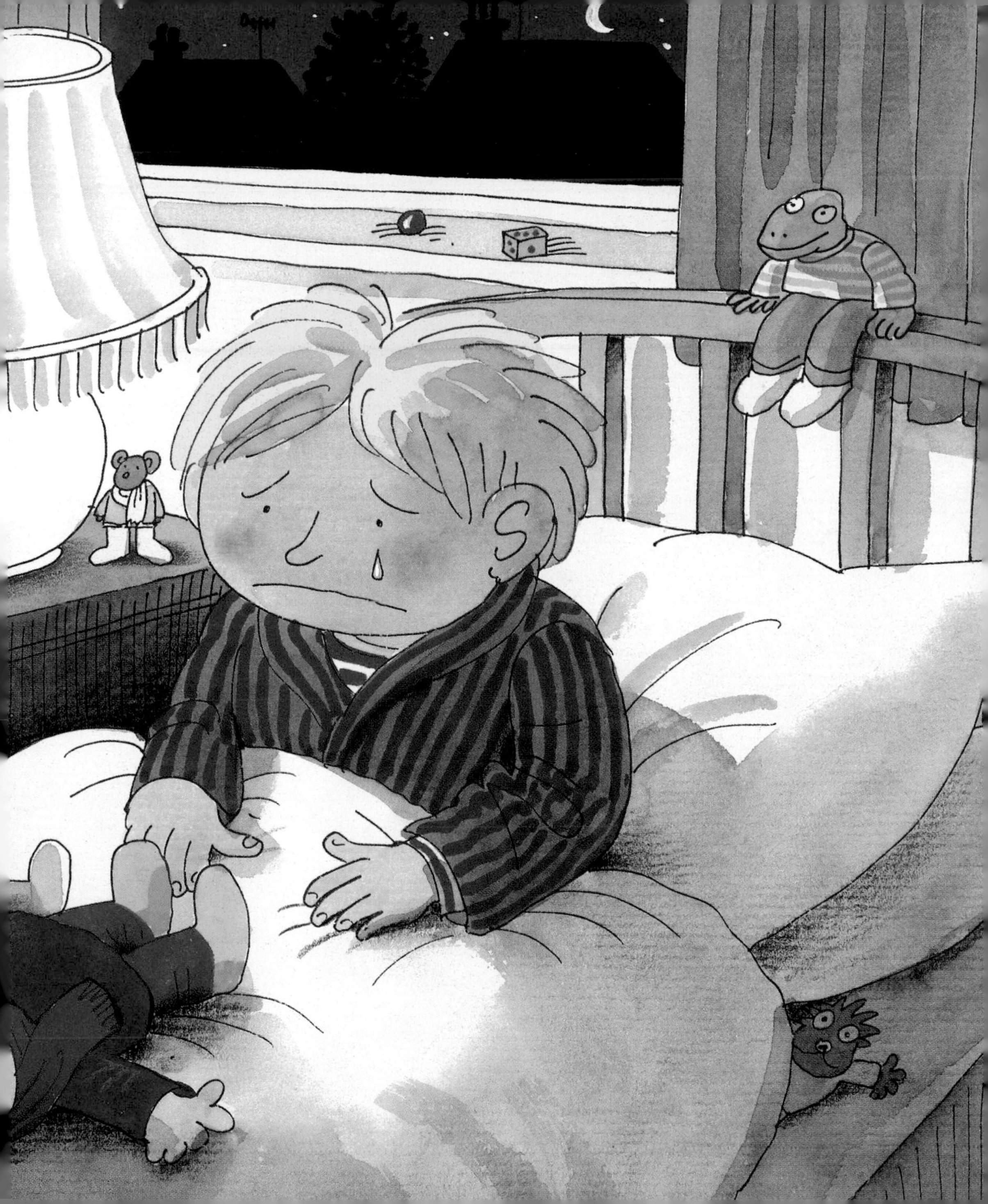

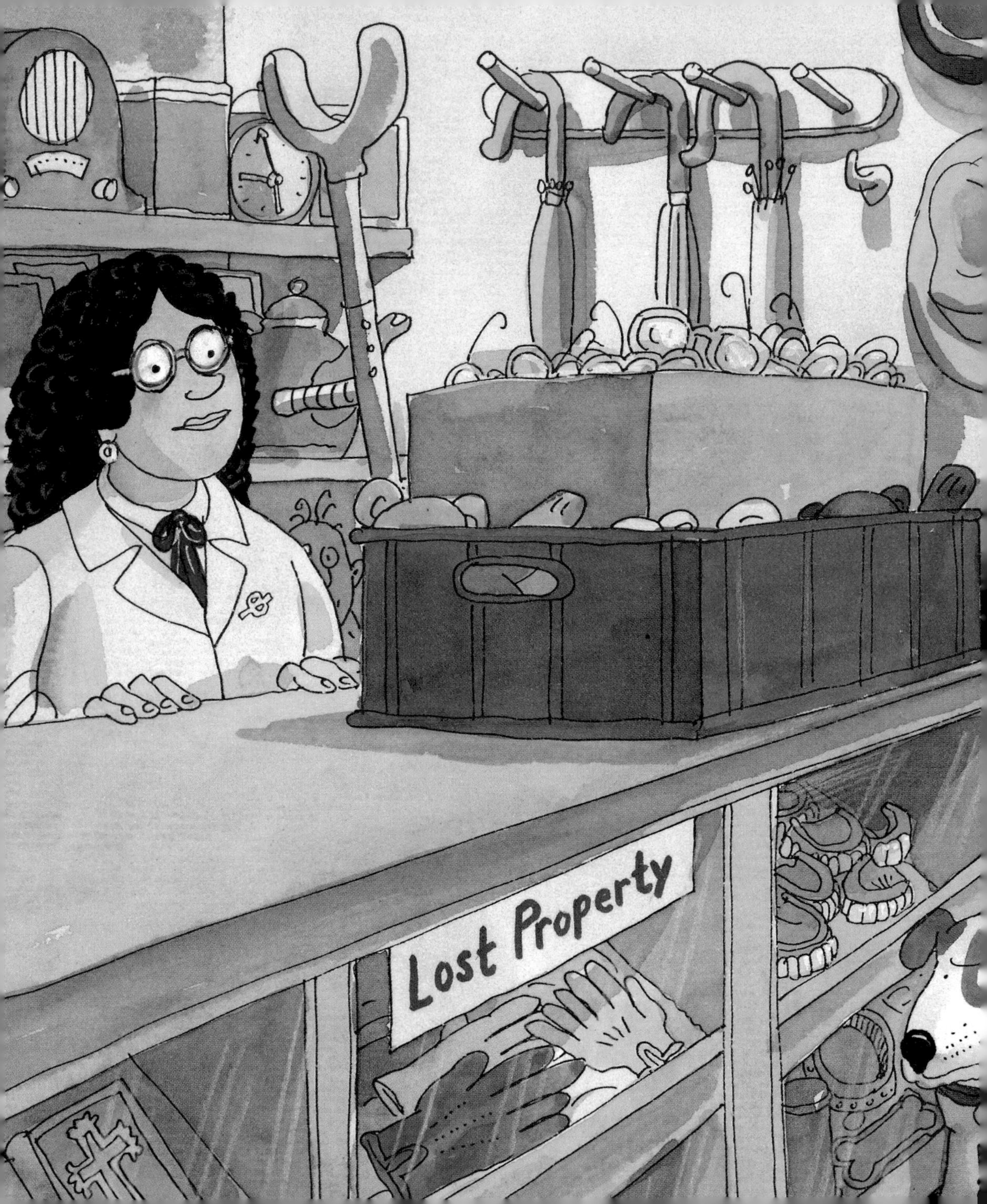
Lost Property

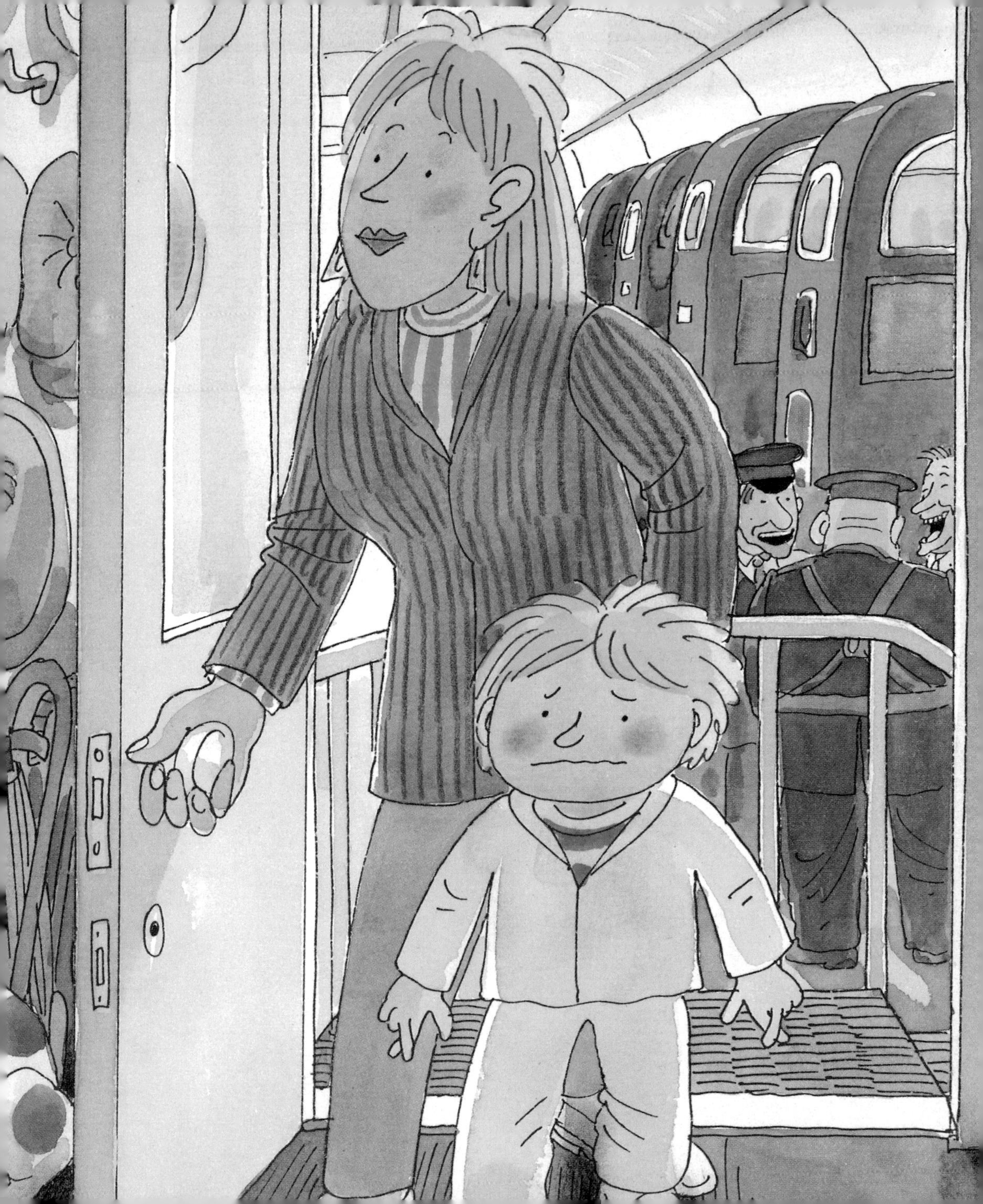

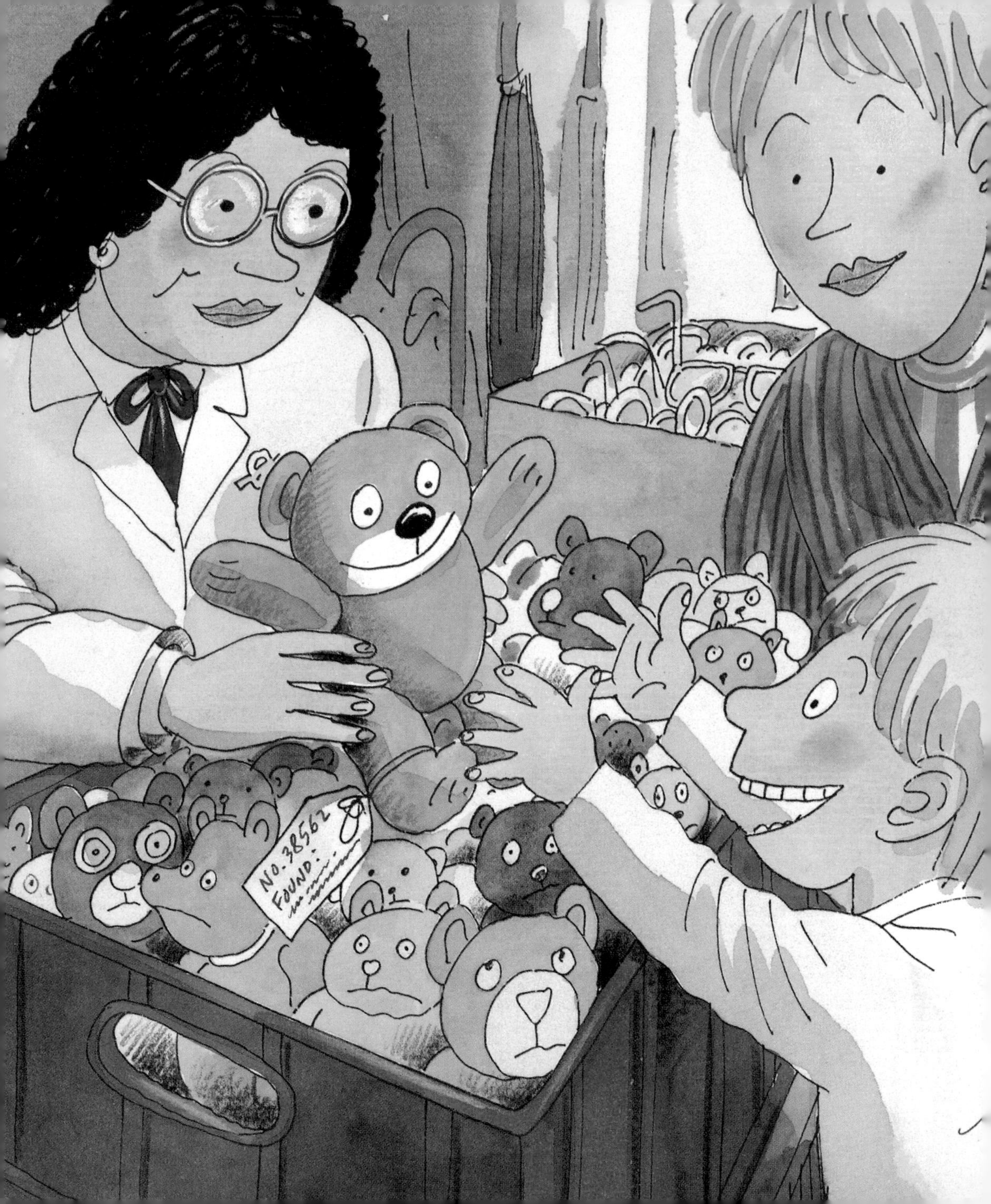
NO. 38562
FOUND: